About the Authors

I am the Cockney Poet who started writing poetry in school. I'm also involved in lots of art and writing groups in my community. I volunteer for various events. I am the chairman at the Chadwell heath community centre.

I am the Dagenham Dame, I started writing poetry
recently when I attended the local writing group in
Chadwell Heath. I learnt writing poetry from Kevin
Walton as it was always a struggle. I never knew how to
start them and now, I can't stop. I hope I am an
example to show it can be done if you practice.
I split my time between going to the cinema I'm
there most of my time and as well as the gym.

We are both from Dagenham RM8!

The Rise of RM8

Kevin Walton and Sky Kelly

The Rise of RM8

Olympia Publishers
London

www.olympiapublishers.com
OLYMPIA PAPERBACK EDITION

A CIP catalogue record for this title is
available from the British Library.

ISBN: 978-1-80074-438-7

First Published in 2022

Olympia Publishers
Tallis House
2 Tallis Street
London
EC4Y 0AB

Printed in Great Britain

Dedication

I dedicate this book to my wife, Jayne Walton, and my daughter, Lara Walton.
Also to Liza Vallance and Cathy Thorley and to everybody that knows me.
I would like to dedicate this book to my mum and dad Susan and Stephen Kelly, my brother, Sam, and his partner, Amber. As well as the rest of my family.

Acknowledgements

Thank you everyone who donated to make this book even become possible. (You know who you are).
We appreciate the help of everybody that made the journey with us. We hope you all enjoy our finished work and hopefully relate to some of our poems.

Silence

Silence
Is an echo I crave
Silence
Is welcome in my grave
Serenity
Is the peace to my rest Serenity
Is life at its best
Calm
Is how I like to feel
Calm
Is the skin I now peel
Relaxed
Is the utopia of living Relaxed
Is the vibe I am giving
Awake
My head explodes and fries Awake
I will tell you no lies

Asleep
My mind stops and becomes brave Asleep
Is the silence that I crave

Gissa Job

I always wanted to be a pugilist
Until I got punched on the nose
So, I tried to be a ballet dancer
But fell because of my stubby toes

I thought I'd become a gynaecologist
But women wouldn't let me look
SO, I tried my hand at being a priest
But didn't like reading their book
I then wanted to be a secret agent But I couldn't follow
secret rules SO I thought I'd become a gardener But I
didn't have any garden tools

I'd give a go at being a florist
But didn't get on with the bees
SO, I tried to be a pet groomer
But got fed up itching from the fleas
I then tried being a ping pong player
But ended up flinging the bat
I even tried being a pole dancer But had trouble because
of my fat

I tried my hand at teaching paragliding But I flew straight

into a tree
SO I thought I'd be a coffee taster But remembered I only
drink tea

I once became a kids' party clown But they didn't laugh at
my act
SO I became a door to door coalman But ended up
getting the sack
I once was a journalist
But I couldn't really spell
SO I joined the cast of T.OW.I.E But wasn't orange
enough, well jell

I tried being a T.V. weatherman
Had trouble finding England on the map
SO, I tried my hand at being a barman
But couldn't get the bottle of the cap
Eventually I thought I'd be a singer
But I couldn't even sing
SO, I became a husband to my wife
When I presented her with a ring?

I then became a loving father
To a beautiful talented daughter
My only job that was left to do
Was walk her down the aisle

BOO

Don't look in the wardrobe Don't look under your bed
Don't look in the cellar
Look at me instead
Don't look in the bathtub Don't look under the stairs
Don't look in the attic
You'll give yourself the scares
Don't look out the window Don't look in the loo
Don't look in the garden Something might just go
BOO!

Innocence lost

When I grow up
What will I become? A teacher
A doctor
A singer
Or even a mum

When I grow up
What will I become? An astronaut
A policeman
A nurse
Or even a nun
When I grow up
What will I be?
A deep-sea diver
A rally driver
A care worker
Or even do surgery

When I grow
What will I be?
A banker
A butcher
A fireman
Or even a secretary

But I will never grow up or grow old Because a man came in standing bold And in our classroom pulled out his gun Killed us all and then his self when done

I will never again see my mum and dad Who every minute since have been sad?

I will never get bigger, and I'll never know The feeling again of sun, rain, or snow

Why, oh why, did that man shoot us all He picked on the innocent and the small All of us children can't show no more love But we all look down from heaven above

Mask within

The person you meet is not me I use it as a false identity
It hides my sorrow and my pain
It is strong enough to take the blame
My real persona is really weak And has forgotten how to
speak But the outgoing face I now use Is protecting my
burnt-out fuse
I am drowning on the inside From the tears I haven't cried
I should have died by now
And taken my final bow
But the main reason I survive Is my loving daughter and
wife The love that they both give Is the reason I still live

Feel

I feel overwhelmed
I feel emotional
I feel insignificant
And I feel very small
I feel insecure
I feel obsolete
I feel anxious
And I feel incomplete
I feel depressed
I feel enraged
I feel dispirited
And I feel disengaged
I want to feel joyful
I want to feel excited
I want to feel happiness But mainly I feel blighted
I want to feel elated
I want to feel contented
I want to feel jubilant But mainly I feel prevented

My mental health is gonna relent And my anxiety and panic subside I am going to start enjoying my life And to this I must and will abide

Pretend

They thought that they were safe here Destitute and
outcasts, alone without fear
The shack was dusty, dank, and very dark And in the
distance, they heard a dog bark
They hankered down way under a chair And became as
quiet as they dare
The door flew open with a loud bang In walked Beverly
and her doo gang
Who is hiding away in my shed she cried? But the bum
cracks are all she espied
Come out now boys, it's time for tea We will carry on
tomorrow at three

The chair

She sits on her white flowered brass chair Reminiscing the
years she had known Putting on her make-up of lipstick
and rouge And brushing her grey hair, always alone

Highs of being a famous film and TV star
Travelling the world with style and grace
Living the good life with fellow actors
And loving everybody knowing her face
She had enjoyed her role on a TV soap Where she played
the tart with a heart But not as glamorous as on the big
screen So, she resigned unhappy with her part

But all that fame was way in the past
And she sits in front of her mirror alone
Nobody comes calling or visiting anymore
To her dilapidated crumbling home
Tears roll down her creased rosy cheeks Her mind in a
whirlwind of faces past Judy Garland presented with an
Oscar But fame and fortune doesn't really last

She smooths her hair and wipes her eyes And smiles

faintly at her faded reflection Picking up the teacup that she had poisoned Waiting for the call of her prompt for action

The papers placed a small memory column About the death of an old English actress Who apparently took her own life? Because of loneliness and her lives stress

This dying earth

The pen is mightier than the sword But mightier is the
spoken word Many a war has been started
And next is world war the third
They signed decrees of peace And swore to adhere to the
rules But nobody ever keeps their words Because leaders
are stupid fools
To stop a war, they use weapons Which really do not work
The world is slowly in demise And nature's dying in the
murk
Innocent people daily being killed On a nightly and hourly
basis All the populations should unite And make the
despots face this
So, everybody needs to take heed Of the death of our
planet
We have to save our earth
And now is the time GODDAMNIT!

Snail

Slowly, slowly, slowly
The snail goes on his way
Slowly, slowly, slowly
It is taking him a day
Slowly, slowly, slowly
No getting out of breath

Slowly, slowly, slowly
Slime is all that's left
Slowly, slowly, slowly
Don't know why he has to roam
Slowly, slowly, slowly
Because on his back is his home

Toddlers

Oh, dear what's that noise
Lots of screaming
And it's not the boys
Oh, dear it's the girls
Who come near?
With their curious curls
Oh, dear they want a kiss It's not for me
I'll give it a miss
Oh, dear ones chasing me I fall down
And graze my knee
Oh, dear she helps me up Gives me a drink
Of which I sup
Oh, dear I've changed my mind I kiss her
And it's nice I find

Oh, dear I want some more But she runs off
To get kisses galore

I don't remember

I don't remember
The thirtieth of December For that's the day I was born
I've also forgot
Quite a lot
Because of this dementia
To pick up a cup
And have a sup
Is something I can't remember
I don't remember
Because of dementia
My name or even my age
I see a beautiful lady
Who loved me once maybe? Perhaps in the past of mine
I sit here and wallow
Forgetting to swallow
All empty and hollow
Waiting to remember

But I don't remember Most thoughts are a blur My mind
lost in dementia And nothing causes a stir
I don't remember
.... Ah so sorry ......
I've forgot

Thirteen

Standing alone with his hands in his pockets Pockets full
of empty holes
Scuffed trousers covered with patches Childhood with no
future goals
Wondering why he is isolated and lonely A black sheep in
the family flock
Thinking there's nothing to look forward to Hands
moving fast on his life clock
His only friend is his imagination A friend to protect him
in life
Retreating into himself and sleeping The new persona
taking the strife
Contemplating death and suicide
Is what no thirteen-year-old should think But the life he
has been dealt with Makes him ready to lay down and sink

Met

I once met the easter bunny
Who plied me with chocolate eggs?
But because of my gluttoness
He took away my legs
I once met Jack Frost
Who tried to help me chill? But I got very angry
When he presented me with his bill?

I once met the tooth fairy
Who looked into my mouth? He saw it was a mess
So, he decided to move south
I once met the sandman
Who tried to help me sleep But my bedroom got packed
Because of the counted sheep

I then met father Christmas Who handed me a gift?
But I didn't say thank you
So, he stormed of in a tiff

Lost times

Balmy nights, kids playing run outs
Time to go home when it gets dark
Boys and girls playing British bulldog
Tagging each other and having a lark
French skipping with large elastic bands 1,2,3 tennis balls
against the wall Playing jacks on the front doorstep Only
stopping when for natures call
Football and cricket daily we'd play Come rain or wind or
snow
And when we didn't have a ball We'd play slappsies all in a
row
No health and safety were ever needed As we climbed and
jumped the sheds Cut and bruises only bothered us When
we'd wince getting into beds
After school the next day
A jubbly we'd all share
Then we played spin the bottle Or a game of truth or dare

We'd play games with our imagination No electronics
entered our heads
For back then most were leaders
And nobody was easily led

Respect and manners we all obeyed And never chatted
back to our mums Cause when dad came in from work
His belt would leather our bums
But these days it's all changed Social media is now today's
boss And our youth have lost their way Which is why the
world is at a loss

English summer

Quick, quick mum the sun is coming out
Get on the phone and give the family a shout
Dads on his way, to get everyone a drink
Aunties washing glasses standing at the sink

My sisters got the BBQ out of the shed
And my older brother has now got out of bed
Shorts and t-shirts, are what they all wear
My mum is in the hallway giving me a stare
She tells me to get in and stop being rude Suddenly I look
down and realise I am nude In all the excitement, I forget
to get dressed I better hurry up, dads back from his quest
The food is now on, and drinks are flowing Family and
friends are coming and going
This is what English summers should be like
Everybody laughing at sleeping sunburnt Mike
Loud laughter and chatter soon fill the air
My dad now sitting in his favourite chair
The paddling pool is now all set up
First one in, is our little staffie pup

Time is late, we are ready to say goodbye And wake adults
who had some shut eye Picking their coats up from off
the floor Hoping the sun will come again once more

Our town

Folk of times gone by
Knew of Barking and Dagenham And the notorious who
lived there Who didn't give a damn?
For no rhyme or reason
Of crimes throughout centuries Stilled within the soul of
man Was murder and robberies
First was Thomas Bonham
A lawyer of the crown
Who defrauded all around?
And then got sent down
There was also P.C Clark
Who got killed on his first day? Rumours abounded and
are unsolved Because the dead can't say
It also has a heritage
Of the famous and the good Residents who changed
opinions Of this distressed Essex hood

A mention must be given
To the farmer William Ford Who donated ten thousand
pounds For a school with bed and board
Gandhi also came and visited And was welcomed at
Kingsley Hall He didn't utter a single word But locals still
held a ball
Capt John Perry and Eva Hart Came from out of our
reach
She had survived the Titanic
And he created Dagenham breach
The man known as the gentleman Was footballer Bobby
Moore Loved on and off the pitch Now goes down in
local folklore
There is more to our district Other than stories of crime
Some of the great people
From this borough of mine

The Dream

Two roads diverged in a yellow wood It was time to say
goodbye
Take care she said
and bowed her head
It was then he started to cry
He met her again and took her hand
They danced slowly throughout the night
But in the morning, she had to leave He watched til she
was out of sight
Kissing under the light of a million stars Laying cuddling
on a cool cut lawn Light disappeared, his view was cleared
A flower then arose from the dawn
And he saw her again in his restless sleep
Diving under and around the unknown
He's swimming about in the deep
Of the greatest love he has never known

Abuse

Fragmented images flicker through my disjointed mind
Of people who abused physically kids of my kind
Latch key children who lived on estates of concrete pride
when confronted with the truth, deep inside they died
Years of buried torment, never believing it happened to
them
Apologies and shame presenting itself to the older men
Whose confidence is shattered remembering bad times
Society not seeing or understanding their facial mimes
We can only deal with the hand we were dealt with Not
displaying to others the loving, we try to give Addiction of
life never caressing in days when low
Wondering if our lives were untouched what would we
show

Change is

Change is
Shrapnel is in the bottom of my pocket Cuts not stinging
me in my dreams Happiness finally showing his face Peace
and harmony whatever that means

Art is
A canvas with a multiverse of colour Sculptures using
their perception of art People discussing the state within
Several not knowing where to start
Change is
Youth of today creating tomorrow Elderly seeing their
world collapsed Food banks and homeless multiplying
Civilisation ready to thrive and
not relapse
Art is
Seeing through the eyes of others Looking around and
noticing change Connecting with people who are different
Utilising the subject is strange

Waiting

What are you waiting for?
Said the sea to the shore
Asked the hinge to the door And the apple to its core
What are you waiting for?
Asked the slipper to the sock Said the doorbell to the
knock And the stir fry to the wok
What are you waiting for?
Nothing really, I'm sitting still Gonna swallow my daily pill
And please to refer to me as bill
Shakespeare was the name I went by Everybody knew of
me before Then Roald Dahl came along A comeback I'm
waiting for

Seasons

Wind sweeps in and blows dead leaves along Rain to
continues to pour soaking our souls Darkness creeps up
quicker and more slyly Autumn attacks our human fragile
bones
Winter has started and mankind's not ready First
snowflakes causing utter chaos
White blanketed rooftops appear on the horizon Lonely
footprints in the crisp white snow
Spring brings the first flowers to bloom Slightly warmer
days and lighter nights Insects awake from their winter
slumber And colour appears on our lives again
Heat wraps us and some people still complain Summers
upon and most are smiling BBQs and food waft by on the
breeze Laughter of children fill the air

Time

It's because of you and what you did That I am writing
this angry rhyme My therapist upon uncovering this Said
it happened and now it's time
Time to remember my hidden past And all the times you
preyed on me Times that you used and abused me The
reason why I am so melancholy
My childhood ruined by a paedophile Because at the time
I was so young And didn't know really what that was
When you kissed me with your tongue?
I was a helpless innocent child That you took full
advantage of Nobody around to protect me I was like a
flame to your moth

You knew it was wrong what you done Plying me with
trips and sweets Groping me whilst driving your car On
silent narrow country streets

It's time for me to stop being ashamed Somebody should
have seen the danger But when you are the black sheep I
am scared and filled with anger
You got away with abuse at the time And for forty years I

was lost

I have hidden and held my childhood My youth is what it cost

Time that I will never get back I was a lonely angry young man Lost years have made me stronger And I cope the best I can

You were the bogeyman I hid away I can't remember your name still But I hope your dead and buried And you were really no

Flim flam man

The flim flam man
Is knocking on our door All last night
And the night before

The flim flam man
Is peeping through the letterbox Mum won't answer
She said we all have the pox
The flim flam man
Is shouting at the house
Mum has told us
To be as quiet as a mouse
The flim flam man
Is apparently very scary
He has four eyes
And is very hairy
We never see the flim flam man Because we always hid
He was the real bogeyman
When I was a kid

But when I got older I realised who he became He was
the provident man And Stanley was his name

Alley

The dark dank alley looked threatening
The mell of strong urine stings my nose
Unable to see around the corners
Lights casting scary looking shadows
Cold grey concrete slabs riddled with dirt
Broken chunks strewn here and there
Silence is attacking all my senses
Anxiety and panic hit me everywhere

My breathing becomes rapid and deep
Sweat streams down my face
I'm struggling to even move on
But I need to exit this place
For behind me lurking in shadows
Is a breast feeding on the weak?
I'm never going back down that alley
I tell myself in a high-pitched squeak

(All above poems by the Cockney Poet aka Kevin Walton)

Persona

I'm fighting for my persona it's always reshaping
pulled in all directions and there's no escaping

So many different crowds some quiet some loud some
extroverts
some introverts
I'm fighting for my persona

But where do I fit?
My personalities split changing my style
to match their profile
I'm protecting my persona

But it's never enough whether I'm weak or tough happy or
sad
good or bad
funny or serious
lucid or delirious
early or late
awful or great
smart or thick
slow or quick
lazy or athletic
cynical or poetic
honest or a lair
defeatist or a Trier quiet or outspoken complete or broken
Brave or scared
damaged and repaired loved or hated
calm or frustrated I'm finding my persona

I look in the mirror they've left marks under the surface
glows noxious remarks
I'm losing my persona

Until I decided
to suffer no more because standing out is what I was born
for I'm saving my persona

Santa's Downfall (part 1)
It was Christmas Eve

Comes around quick we all believe
Santa was doing his rounds
his feet not touching the ground

he looks up
the Easter Bunny was inches away wearing Santa's backup
costume leaning on Santa's sleigh

he smokes his last cigarette
the length of a baguette
the tooth fairy by his side
they look liked Bonnie and Clyde

Santa has to play dumb
if he wants to get out of this
"Is that a new suit?"
He knows his taking the piss

What are you two doing here?
It's the wrong time of year
so get back in your hole
or tomorrow you'll get coal!"

"You still owe me my money "
and you've kept me waiting
you've had all year
you see how that's frustrating?"

"Consider this payment
I'll deliver the toys
I've said what I needed
now get him boys!"

The elves surround him
knocking him out with a candy cane throwing the sack
over his head tying his feet with Rudolph's rein

Hogtied and gagged
throwing him in the boot
"Make sure he can't get out Cause in the air is a lawsuit!"
Santa finally comes around
he's locked in a suitcase
The tooth fairy shrunk him down so he's got enough
space

He was really scared

he didn't know what to do
but he didn't realize
he followed through

he hears the Easter Bunny laughing
and the elves celebrating
getting taken out by them
is just humiliating

he thinks he's the big man
Enjoy this while you can
cause when I'm out of here you better disappear

Russell (part 2)

With one loud bang
Santa rolled out of the suitcase he was balancing on the
chimney so he landed on his face

"That fucking rabbit
and his poxy habits!"
he unties the ropes setting him free he sees piss running
to his knees

In the bushes down below
Santa hears a rustle
crawling in the snow
it's his elf Russell

he been tied up
blindfolded and gagged
there was a trail behind
from where he'd been dragged

Santa jumps from the roof and unties Russell
he was tied up tight
so it was quite the tussle

"That bloody rabbit
has gone too far
he drank all my whiskey
and smoked my cigar!"

"I tried to warn ya
but they jumped me
bunch of traitors
even that bastard McCredie!"

Santa leans on the fence
and lights up his blunt
Russell stretches out his hand
so hands him one with a grunt

"I need new trousers
before we do anything
I pissed and shat myself
and now my arse stings"

"Alright fine
do you have a plan?"
"Of course I do
we go back to where it began"

An Ally You Can Rely On (part 3)

Santa calls a trusted ally
"Right, he says he's on his way"
Russell remains apprehensive
"Yeah, let's hope and pray"

"He'll be here
He's just a bit slow"
and within seconds
a button hits Santa's toe

It's Frosty the snowman
smoking his pipe
with his favourite scarf on
the one with the stripes

"About time you showed up!" "Shut up you lil clown

I was in the night club
on the other side of town"

"Thank you Frosty
it's an emergency
that's why I called
with such urgency"

"No problem, Santa
you helped me out
that time when I was in the club and I called the owner a
trout"

"Anyway, what's the plan? I'll help however I can"
"Well, the sleigh has a tracker with Russell being a hacker

"He'll hack the system
until it loses control
the system will crash
sending Bunny in the hole

"It'll take careful timing
but it will work
And when it does
it'll wipe away that smirk"

"So why do we need Frosty?" "Cause he's our ride there"
"I'll grab the broomstick "And not Claire the polar bear"
"Sounds good boss"
"Right grab our suits
cause right now
There's an arse waiting for my boot"

Back to the North Pole (part 4)

The three of them ride a broomstick
Frosty borrowed it from the witch
"We have to get there quick
this thing has a tendency to glitch"

they land at the North Pole
there's not a soul in sight
not exactly surprising
It's possible to get frostbite

Easter bunny flies above them
he's back to collect more supplies
"How does anyone think he's me?
Look at his poor disguise!"

"Are you ready Russell?"
"Wait something's wrong"
"What are you talking about?"
"It shouldn't take this long"

There was a loud commotion behind
Mrs Clause is looking for more tequila
she's finished a bottle by herself
it was a gift from her friend Sheila

Mrs Clause comes out
ranting and raving
they all knew she was drunk
by the way she's behaving

Bunny watched the whole thing his attention now
elsewhere
he is to mesmerised
seeing Mrs Clause in her outerwear

He crashes in to the tower and it goes up in flames
"Well, the good news is
I can make a lot of claims"

He crawls in the snow
trying to escape
but Santa stops him
stepping on his drape
"All right all right I give up I'll disappear and never come
back just let me grab my stash
it's tucked in my backpack"

"No, I owe you
and you'll get it back
once I've got it
I'll leave it in your shack"

"I think we all need a drink after all this shit"
"Though it was quite funny I have to admit"

"Everyone's at the bar
Jack Frost is inside
He used to be a good kid
before he became a snide"

"Oh, don't be mad at the elves I paid them all off
and not to breathe a word or even a cough"

"let's get this party started and forget this nightmare"
"Oh, one more thing, Santa will your Mrs Clause be
there?"

Is Blood Thicker Than Water?

Is blood thicker than water?
Two siblings will decide
a fight led to this
by the one who always lied

Their ghosts hover over
their old, cracked tomb
it was hard to believe
they shared the same womb

They stand by the old tree
where they used to play
the sweat pouring off their face
one will die again today

refusing to shake their feelings
The memories remain there
The brothers hold the gun
Pull the trigger do they dare

both eyes daring one another
"Please, put down your gun"
he ignored his request
The relationship was done

There is no going back
the betrayal runs too deep
his final words to him
"My bullet will put you to sleep"

they remain stuck
in an endless time, loop
because they can't bury the grudge that shattered their
outlaw group

Shots were fired
the crows flee the scene
the fog clears to reveal
both bodies buried back in the green

After You've Gone

It was only after he'd gone her life finally began
he chased and chased her
shouting I'm your biggest fan!

She played one character
and he thought she was her The real her doesn't exist
she is now just a blur

his wife no longer had her identity he ruined her serenity
from all the role-playing
for her safety she was praying

the constant harassment
the endless letters he sent
and if she never replied
her car would have a dent

she slept with one eye open and a weapon by her bed
she'd look to her door with dread the sweat dripping from
her head

constantly asking herself
was it something I said?
he drove her to drugs
she bought off local thugs
he drove her to smoke
enough for her to choke
he drove her to drink
she had weekly visits to a shrink

she sat in the car
and patiently waited
what she's about to do
she constantly debated

he left the theatre
looking down at his phone
smiling away to himself
her presence unbeknown
she did have second thoughts
Can I really take your life?
What about your friends and family? And what about your
wife?

Fuck it!

putting her foot down

the tyres screeched
her eyes in the interior mirror showed the desperation
she's reached

Enough was enough
he was hit by the car
flying completely over
the directors Jaguar

his body cracked the window as he flew over the top
the blood poured down
dripping like raindrops

this could have been prevented
had he had left her alone
but he was too dangerous from the obsession he'd shown

driving home
ignoring the red lights
ignoring the flashing blue lights ignoring the flashing
amber lights ignoring the flashing green lights

she walked past her security they gave a friendly nod
from all her shivering

did they not find that odd?

Unlocking the door to her flat she collapsed to the floor
leaning on her door
not dealing with him anymore

did it have to be done?
Now I'm not so sure
much like her character
she also became impure

The 7 Arts Of You (Music, Art, Sculpture, Writing, Stage,
Architecture & Cinema)
To me
Music has no noise
because you are the sound
Apollo should hang up his lyre
and have you crowned
to me
A canvas has no art
the colour wheel
has no appeal
until you picked up the brush
and paint the shy heart you conceal
To me
you are Aphrodite's design
beauty in its purest guise
sculpted by virtuous intent

that's forbidden to criticize
to me
you are a poet's dream
A writer's versatility
accepting the good and the bad paths
with such humility
to me

The world's your stage
and you're the luminary
to witness your flair
is evolutionary
To me
you stand tall and proud
weathering every storm
even when you want to collapse you stand on a stronger
platform To me
no visual effects can manipulate the faculty you provide
your motion pictures
should be shown worldwide

A Hero (part 1)

The house appears
when the fog disappears
evil still perseveres
bringing alive everyone's fears

as it sits in the woods
protecting its goods
the soul gem is strife
bringing everyone dead to life

you don't want to be outside especially at nightfall
when the ghost rises again to complete their soul ritual

the bats expand their wings
impressing their dark kings the wonders they'll bring
collecting the eternal ring

the devil sits on the throne watching how destruction is
sewn as the torches are ablaze
the scorching heat burns the haze

the vampires leave their crypts the wolves howl at the
moon gargoyles fly in the sky
the witches fight at the lagoon

the goblins steal
while the mermaid's appeal the skeletons dance
taking every chance

The heroes lay trapped
the angel statue weeps
all they can really do
is watch them sleep

the Greek gods do their best to end this monstrosity
but they block the rays of sun to continue their atrocity
Bellerophon grabs his arrow the one with the gold
sparrow His Pegasus is prepared
for the war that's' been declared

the thunder roars
and the clouds divide
lightning bolts strikes through as good and evil collide

Shooting his shot

the soul gems shatters
watching them all collapse
is all that matters

There is peace once more everything's laid to rest
well until next time
then begin the stress

The Aftermath (part 2)

It been only a few days
since the dead were laid to rest it was Bellerophon mission
to complete this quest

the house that was hidden
needs to stay forbidden
hiding the soul gem
to stop the mayhem

Hecate watched from afar
she knew better than to interfere she'd be with those who
fell
and be dead for years

her magic kept her alive this time
she's still going strong
but it takes a lot of energy
uncertain for how long

Hecate walks the garden
where destruction began

such weak-minded fools
she had a much bigger plan

The gardens back to green
the flowers start to bloom
but that won't last
as the danger looms

Ares waits by the tree
as he too was set free
The underworld had him enslaved with a tombstone
engraved

"I see Hell set you free
that's good to know
those morons have us stuck in a loop working alone is too
slow"

"I have a proposal"
He leans with a smirk
"I know how to bring them back And it won't take much
work"

"We wait till sundown
When it's a ghost town
find the graveyard tomb
concealed in the gloom"

"Turn the sundial back
exactly 24 hours
when they all rise again
the armies will be ours"

the last thing we need
is for these two too lead
they wait by the gates
as hell now awaits

Striking Midnight (part 3)

The clock strikes midnight
the full moon beams
their grins unmissable
reflecting their gleams

the red mist disperses
the church tower is exposed
he turns to Hecate
just as he proposed

the tower doors fling open
the bats fly through
they wait upside down on the trees knowing what they'll
do

they climb the stairs
it overlooks the town
it looks peaceful now
until it drowns

Time rewinds

Ares turns the sundial
this excites him more
then when he was in exile

the ground shakes
the tombstones break
creating ripples in the lakes from the erupting earthquakes

the creatures rise once more from exactly where they fell
their ashes sewn back together from the sundials spell

Ares grabs the soul gem
He knows Bellerophon will return but once he's trapped
he'll no longer be a concern

They stand ready
they know for sure they'll win Ares turns to his army
"Let us begin!"

A Fallen Hero (part 4)

The village's burn for miles
tress burned to the seeds
the moon rotates backwards the deep red it bleeds

Ares and Hecate wait in the dark Bellerophon will be here
soon he has to take him out quick before he sends his
platoon

Pegasus charges through the storm he's right on cue
the gods above will be helpless once he's destroyed their
rescue

he readies his arrow once more
but the soul gem has disappeared it's now missing
it's everything he has feared

Ares throws the flaming sword
it flares through the sky
as the sword approaches
he waits on standby

with the approaching light
Bellerophon catches sight
and with all his might
he pulls on Pegasus tight

Pegasus loses concentration
his wings battle the tornado
Bellerophon loses his grip
knocking off his bow and arrow

his body is weightless
Pegasus cannot catch him
he plummets in to the stone floor tearing apart his limbs

Ambushing Bellerophon
They have his Pegasus restrained he tries to fight them off
but they have him chained

Throwing Bellerophon in the tower the poisonous chains
take his power Pegasus remains defiant
Bellerophon needs him to be compliant

"You'll be here a while"
He said with a vile smile
Bellerophon is under lock and key not believing this
dreaded reality

all he can do is observe

not believing Ares's nerve
One by one they fall
someone helps them all

This Place I Call Home

This place used to be great
now it's somewhere that aggravates nothing but street
fights
under the flickering lights
This place I call home

A place full of drug deals
never knowing their next meal
getting kicked out of a family pub
just to move on to the club
This place I call home

the neighbours want to shriek
weed makes the road reek
there are no restraints
despite all the complaints
This place I call home

the sirens blare in the early hours
racing through a block of towers
helicopters hover over the districts
trying not to add to the statistics
This place I call home

Market traders try flogging their gold rings swearing they
were once worn by kings claiming they are better than
ones in the shops until they have to run from the cops
This place I call home

but it's not always bad
even when we are a bit mad
it has good moments to
a community that always come through This place I call
home

A place where we don't get chances under unfortunate
circumstances we're judged by our postcode not from the
talent we've showed
This place I call home

A place where others claim
they don't tarnish us all the same but you see from their
expression we've left a bad impression
This place I call home

Unrequited

I'm in love with you
and it suffocates me
to my heart all I do is plea
I do my best to move on
and forget I was your liaison

I'm in love with you
I desire you and only you
whether it's on the bed or the floor on the table or drawer
pinned to the walls
of all the halls
from the chairs
on to the stairs
passionate or erotic
gentle or chaotic
I desire you and only you

I shouldn't be in love with you it's mesmerising
it's energizing
it's tantalizing
but it's agonizing
I shouldn't be in love with you

I want to forget you
you were my pathfinder
to a painful reminder
but I still chased you
and met you at every rendezvous I want to forget you

A Cry for Help

It all kicked off
when the best man began his speech he started it off
shouting everyone is a thieving leech

he'd been drinking all day
he couldn't be stopped
he was so adamant
his drinks had been swapped

everyone saw the state he was in a recovering alcoholic
with this show just as all the in-laws sighed
oh boy here we go

so, the scandals begin
he banged her she banged him she wasn't getting it at
home and he refused get slim
she said he's inadequate
with his bedroom skills
he said it was all because
he took the wrong pills
his got a secret family
she's having an affair

their getting divorced
they've got problems with childcare
The newlyweds don't know love the weddings a false
presentation the bride's father is really mad crushing his
glass with frustration She's a gold digger
and now he's skint
everyone here sees it
we've all dropped hints
the groom's ex is here
hiding in the back room
she said the brides a witch I've even found her broom
That's enough out of you! The bride's father charges to
him he trips over the groom's jacket and falls into Uncle
Jim
you fucking clown!
Punching him on the nose flying into the table
knocking him off his toes

the table snaps

and so do the guests
as everyone knows
weddings are tolerant tests

the best man steps outside and starts to cry
collapsing on to the step
weeping I'm not a bad guy

he cries for help
the only way he knows how
by plummeting further down
screaming save me now!

Pulling the strings

I have a love hate relationship with my ventriloquist
master
he only started me up
because he is a washed-up broadcaster

he may pull all my strings
but I own his voice
he does what I say
I don't give him a choice

his hand goes too far up my arse I feel it in my head
So, I turn and whisper to him you're lucky I'm dead

if I did that to him
it'd be a different story
his voice would be so squeaky
it'll cause damage to his respiratory

he pulled a fast one on me
tried cutting me loose
tied all my strings
to a hysterical goose

then he tried setting me on fire but I rolled on to his rug
then I laid there as it burned
and looked at him all smug

When that didn't work
He tried to drown me
He knows I don't have lungs, right?
This clown has a carpentry degree

He tried to embarrass me
By removing my gown
The audience looked disappointed
Because I have nothing downtown

We even drove off a cliff
Had me strapped tight in my car seat
He jumped before we reached the edge
I screamed yeah you better retreat

The car went up in flames
He watched from the ledge
Witnessing my body
Fly into the hedge

I throw my fists to him
I'm still here you arsehole
I see the stressed I've caused
Has now taken its toll

I slam the door behind me
He is rocking in his chair
Should we call a truce
Yeah, I think that's fair

Rise the Purple Moon

Once again
The purple moon rises
We have theories on what it symbolises
But what no one realises
Is the beauty it disguises

In the hot pink sky
It peacefully blends
Looking almost ghostly
But it's message still sends

The deep blue sea   .
Keeps its calming effect
It's inner peace
It wants to protect

Until the black clouds come
Shadowing its light
Until no longer visible
Shaming it out of spite

Thunder erupts
Pouring down the rain
Tainting the ground
With poisonous stains

Since the rise of the dark
The sea loses control
The turbulent tides crash
Darkening its soul

The sky transitions
From pink to red
Without permission
Hatred has spread

People watch hopelessly
As it painfully deteriorates
Suffering in the silence
Of this negative weight

The stars continue to glimmer
Shining rays of hope
No matter how dire it gets
It still has strength to cope

Then realisation hits.......

No matter how hard
Its tries to hide
The purple is unique
So, shine with pride

The purple moon beams
Stronger than before
Its inner strength
Surfacing from the core

Burning away the dark
A pink mist consoles
As it knows evil
Has left cynical holes

Returning your heart

I'm retuning your heart
For its not meant for me
I don't return your love
So let me set you free

I'd walk past you
And go about my day
Unbeknown to me
You felt this way

Please don't blame yourself
I'm not the one for you
My feelings remain still
While your feelings grew

Someone else will love you
The way I never could
And it will feel right
Just the way it should

I know feelings can be strong
Addicted to powerful lust
But this won't go any further
Let me go you must

I know for a fact
You'd treat me like royalty
Nothing would tempt you away
And betray my loyalty

It hurts me too
Not feeling the same
I get no satisfaction
Watching you ache in pain

The Chemistry of an Introvert

I was never one to believe
In love at first sight
But when I met you
Something felt right

From the second I saw you
The chemistry was there
For me to feel this way
Is extremely rare
Logic scatters everywhere

Being the introvert, I am
I kept my distance
I tried to ignore it
It held me with persistence
My heart was at resistance

It was hard to keep my eyes off you
But I knew I had too
I didn't think I stood a chance
So, I didn't catch your glance
As I knew my feelings would enhance

So, I turned away
To go about my day….
Then you came over and said hello
And just like that time was slow
The air stopped in my torso
My head suffered vertigo
From this internal tornado
My tongue was tied
Unravelling it I tried
But I was just mystified
From a smile so wide
My blushing I couldn't hide
As my hot and cold sweat collides
And with that I replied……
"Hi"

Bullet proof vest

I want to be
Your bullet proof vest
To stop the bullets
From reaching your chest

I want to be
Your strongest shield
The sword you wield
On the battlefield

I want to be
Your bullet proof vest
To protect you
From the distress

I want to be
The antidote to your bane
To take away the pain
And see you smile again

I want to be
Your bullet proof vest
To save your heart
from cardiac arrest

I want to be
The cure to your disease
Even if it means
Bringing me to my knees

I want to be
Your bullet proof vest
Till my dying breath
Puts me to rest

Try

Give me a try
I might surprise you
Let my actions prove
That what I say is true

Your needs will be a priority
Always be my number one
Cause with you in my arms
I know I've won

Always have my attention
No problem is big or small
If you feel your world collapsing
I'll catch you when you fall

I'll never play mind games
I'll never string you along
Or have you thinking you're to blame
Or questioning if you were wrong

In more ways than one
I'll spoil you in every way
Not just with gifts
I know that sounds cliché

No secrets
No hidden agenda
To be honest with you
Not a lying pretender

But you know your worth
Cause that is essential
You're special without me
With so much potential

Give me a try
Prove to you I'm unique
I won't let you down
And hope I'm everything you seek

Racing the Inferno

The metropolis burned
It brightens up the sky
The scorching flames
Ignited so high

The people fled
The animals too
Racing the inferno
The faster it grow

The blazing orange
Illuminates the night
Despite its destruction
It was quite a sight

How did this happen
Everyone was shaken
Looking into the distance
Praying no one was taken

The enraged sky above
Rained down the ashes
Circling the civilians
As it lightly crashes

Caught up in the air
Is thick black smoke
It shows no mercy
As the people choke

Who is that in the distance?
Is that a man?
Overlooking the destruction
He's been there since it began

A dark figure stands
On top of the hill
With a match in his hand
He's out for the kill

Please don't call me

Please don't call me
Never again anymore
It was all over
When you closed the door

When trouble was thick
You turned away
Now it's over
You have lots to say

Please don't call me
With more of your lies
I see through them now
Learning from you made me wise

You fooled me before
And that's down to me
Cause I ignored the red flags
For you to continue rent free

Please don't call me
I'm now done
In my heartache
You had your fun

Pulling me in
With "I love you"
Your feelings were static.
While my feeling grew

I never needed you
It was you who needed me
But you convinced me otherwise
Your hold wouldn't let me see

Releasing your grasp
I am now free
It's for the best
We both will agree

Home

I know I'm home
The smell of piss in the air
I know I'm home
People leave behind their underwear
I know I'm home
The smell of weed chokes us all
I know I'm home
When conversations end in a brawl
I know I'm home
When the cat's mate in the street
I know I'm home
Their fur is left in the streets
I know I'm home
The foxes fight over their prey
I know I'm home
Cause they crap in the archway
I know I'm home
When the neighbours begin karaoke
I know I'm home
The smokers' voices are all chokey
I know I'm home
The street fights begin
I know I'm home
One gets knocked on the chin

I know I'm home
When the boy racers compete
I know I'm home
Graffiti is sprayed on the concrete
I know I'm home
When disasters on the news
I know I'm home
It's a message from the boys in blue
I know I'm home
When merchants flog their gold
I know I'm home
Their chains are something to behold

Followed by my Ghost

The ghost that follows me
Are my past mistakes
The ghost that haunts me
Is waiting for me to break

The ghost that chases me
Is everything it appears
The ghost that scares me
Has combined all my fears

The ghost that torments me
Is all the things I should never had said
The ghost that judges me
Is seeing vengeful red

The ghost that likes to remind me
I've done bad things
The ghost that likes to embarrass me
Puppets them on strings

The ghost that suffocates me
Stops the air in my throat
The ghost that stares into my eyes
Knows forgiveness hold the antidote

The ghost that questions me
Waits for my replies
The ghost that waits for me
Won't accept my lies

The ghost that confronts me
Wants me to be tough
The ghost that supports me
Know life can be rough

The ghost that forgives me
Is finally done
The ghost that says goodbye
Believes my future has begun

(all poems above by Sky Kelly)

Year of Fear

And so, the world turned
It was without warning
The human race had burned
From night till the morning

Isolated people worry all day
Their minds climb the walls
Most just sit and pray
But fear and worry crawls

They realised what was missing
Searching high and low
Most just started wishing
That time becomes more slow

Population of earth diminished
But mother nature thrived
And when the planet had finished
It repaired what had been deprived

The land was finally green again
It breathed a sigh of relief
As paradise can now be seen
And finally, no more grief

The virus had slowly passed
Our future wasn't so bleak
Let's hope the unity will last
Cause together we are not weak